The WEAVERS
of ANCIENT PERU

Text and photography by
M.S. Fini, Dip. Textiles, B.A. (Hons.)
of Tumi, Latin American Crafts.

An exhibition of Peruvian textiles
at the
Commonwealth Institute,
London
5th September to 28th October
1985

Published by
Tumi

TUMI

Importers of Latin American Crafts,
London and Bath.

ISBN

0-9511055-0-7

Contents

Front cover from a painting by
a Peruvian street artist.

Illustrated by J. Gwazdacz.

Cartography by J. Abraham.

Studio photograph by R. Laing.

Typeset and printed by Penwell Ltd.,
Parkwood, Callington, Cornwall.

◀ *Birds from Chancay textiles.*

Preface

Some forms of artistic expression have been restricted to particular societies at particular times, whereas others can be found in every society and at all times.

These universal, and oldest, forms are invariably associated with simple, often domestic, needs and aspirations; decoration of the home, clothing and decorating the body, story telling, preparing food and making music—activities which are inseparable from the experience of being alive and part of human society. At their best there is a special quality to these forms of expression that transcends time, place and 'taste', and speaks directly to the soul.

These textiles from Peru—like the Indian Costumes from Guatemala which we exhibited in 1983, the Nigerian Textiles in 1984, or the songs of the Inuit Women which we heard in this year's Ancestral Voices Festival—are fine examples, both traditional and contemporary, of Popular Arts in the truest sense of that expression. They are highly developed, yet completely unpretentious, created by gifted artists who function both as individuals and yet as representatives of the shared values of their society.

Long may these cultural activities and the values they represent survive, both for their own sake and for the influence they may bring to an increasingly fragmented and competitive world.

Robert Atkins (Arts Director)
Emma Wallace (Visual Arts Director)
Commonwealth Institute
London, August 1985

Foreword

An exhibition of Peruvian weaving is a special event. A lot of valuable research has been taking place over the past decades into Peru's artistic heritage, both in Peru and abroad, but this has concentrated mostly on the pre-Colombian achievements, and tended to focus on ceramics more than textiles.

Only a very small selection of items from Peru's immensely rich cultural heritage are on display in the exhibition but it is hoped to show something of the evolutionary process in relation to textiles from pre-Colombian times to the present day.

We all know about the achievements of the great civilisations of the Old World; China, Egypt, Persia and Greece, and their contribution to the advancement of mankind, but there is little appreciation of the achievements of the ancient civilisations of the New World. To look at the fine and skilfully woven threads of a weaving of ancient Peru with its intricacy of design, its rich colour, is to know the countless painstaking minutes and long devoted hours of its making and to understand the sophistication of the culture that produced it. These accomplishments, I believe, should be recognised and seen in their broader, global perspective rather than as distinctly 'New World'.

To understand why there is not more participation in research programmes in Peru, and why exhibitions are few, involves an understanding of the rapid changes taking place in Peru. At the same time research and exhibitions on a large scale are expensive and the resources of Third World countries are indeed very limited. Thus, it is exciting to be fortunate enough to organise a small exhibition like this and to have been privileged with assistance from FOPEX, the Peruvian export office, and the Commonwealth Institute. I am very grateful to both of these institutions for their support.

My hope is that the exhibition will help towards a fuller understanding and appreciation of 'New World' heritage. The book has been written to accompany the exhibition but its emphasis is visual and it is hoped it will thus exist independently of it. I have felt it important to provide some general background as well as looking at those areas of special significance and personal interest such as symbolism and regional tradition.

The exhibition and this book are the result of extensive collaboration with numerous people, with members of co-operative organisations and even entire village communities. Among the people who have really made these possible I would extend my deep gratitude to Senora Gertrud Solari for her interest in the project and above all the generous contribution of her unpublished studies on symbolism. It is a privilege to be able to include them in this work. To the members of the Kamaq Maki co-operative in Huancayo I am much indebted for their worthy efforts in the study of herbal dyes. Likewise the people of San Pedro de Cajas, in particular Sr. Palomino who, together with Sr. Flores from Taquile, have undertaken a long journey from their villages in Peru to come to London for the period of the exhibition to demonstrate their traditional weaving skills. Finally, I would like to thank some of my personal friends, among them Senors Jorge Navorro and Jose Kellor who played an important role in organising material in Peru. I would like to thank Diana Scrafton for her help in preparing the text, Julio Etchart for his encouragement and the contribution of eight lovely photographs, and all my colleagues at Tumi who coped with much extra pressure of work to enable me to undertake the project.

A special thanks goes to my wife Jane, and our young son Cori, for their love and understanding and constant support during the many months of preparation for the exhibition.

Moh Fini, July 1985

Shipibo tribal design painted on a wall in the Pucalpa region of the Peruvian Amazon. It represents the rivers and settlements of the Shipibo territory and appears on their textiles and everyday pottery.

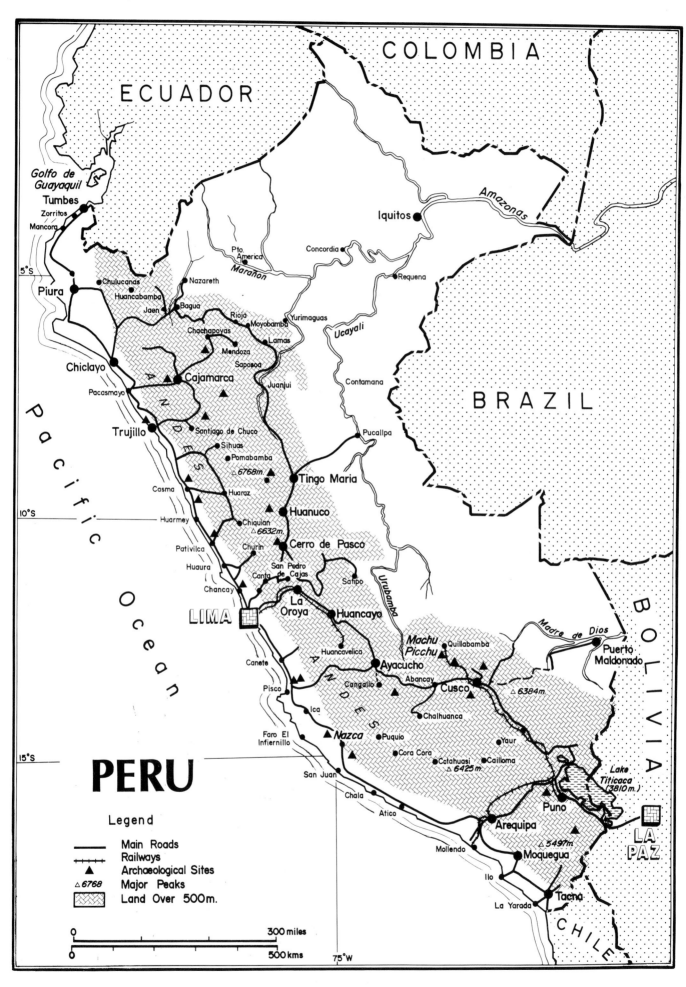

COLOMBIA

ECUADOR

Golfo de
Guayaquil

Tumbes
Zorritos
Mancora

Iquitos

Amazonas

5°S

Piura

Chulucanas
Huancabamba
Jaen
Bagua
Chachapoyas
Mendoza
Saposoa
Lamas

Pto.
America

Concordia

Requena

Marañon

Nazareth

Rioja
Moyobamba

Yurimaguas

Ucayali

Chiclayo
Pacasmayo

Cajamarca

Juanjui

Contamana

BRAZIL

Trujillo

Santiago de Chuco

Sihuas
Pomabamba
△6768m.

Pucallpa

Casma

Huaraz

Tingo Maria

10°S

Huarmey

Chiquian
△6632m.

Huanuco

Pativilca

Churin

Cerro de Pasco

Huaura
Canta

San Pedro
de Cajas

Safipo

Urubamba

Chancay

LIMA

La
Oroya

Huancayo

Madre de Dios

Canete

Huancavelica

*Machu
Picchu*

Quillabamba

Puerto
Maldonado

Pisco

Cangallo

Ayacucho

Abancay

Cusco

△6384m.

BOLIVIA

Ica

Chalhuanca

Faro El
Infiernillo

Nazca

Puquio

Cora Cora

Yaur

15°S

San Juan

Catahuasi
△6425m.

Cailloma

*Lake
Titicaca
(3810 m.)*

PERU

Chala

Atico

Puno

Arequipa

LA
PAZ

Legend

Mollendo

△5497m.

Ilo

Moquegua

Pacific Ocean

—— Main Roads
┼┼┼ Railways
▲ Archaeological Sites
△6768 Major Peaks
▦ Land Over 500m.

La Yarada

Tacna

CHILE

0   300 miles
0   500 kms

75°W

ANDES

An Introduction to the History of Peruvian Textiles

Weaving has been one of the most important activities in the Andean world for thousands of years. Textiles have served many functions for the Indians, and to understand the cultural process of the region is to appreciate that textiles were a fundamental part of the economy, as well as having social and political significance and daily utilitarian value. Weavings were the most highly prized of possessions and the most sought after trading commodity in the Andes during pre-Colombian times. It is therefore not surprising that, despite the decimation of the Indians' social and economic order during the Spanish Conquest, the cultural tradition of weaving has survived up to the present day.

In the Andean world textiles played an important role in political, social and religious ceremony. Gifts of specially woven cloth were used to strengthen social and political bonds, and at burial times the dead were buried with the most precious woven cloth. The exquisite weavings found in the graves of Paracas bear witness to the tremendous importance attached to textiles during burial ceremonies.

The Incas inherited three thousand years of weaving skill and tradition. Virtually all the weaving techniques known to modern man were known to the ancient Peruvians. The weavers knew how to produce a great variety of fabrics from simple plain weaves to quite intricately varied ones, fabrics with supplementary decorative warp and weft yarns, double cloth, gauzes, open-work fabrics, tapestry, and plain cloth weaves decorated with printed and painted surfaces, or tie-dyed. Studies of Andean textiles have concentrated on these pre-Inca developments and much research has been done on the comparatively well-preserved textiles of the coastal cultures of Paracas (700 B.C. - 1100 A.D.), Nazca (100 B.C. - 900 A.D.), Wari (600 -1100 A.D.) and Chancay (100 B.C. - 1200 A.D.).

Paracas mummy.

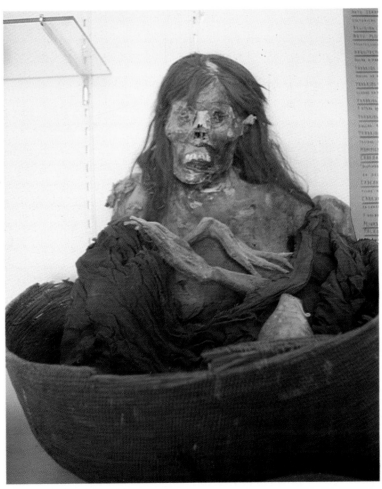

Paracas Culture (700 B.C.- 100 A.D.)

During the ninth century B.C. cameloid fibres were introduced into the weaving of the southern coastal region of Peru, and the first cameloid hair tapestries began to appear in an area which previously had worked solely with human hair and plant fibres. This innovation allowed the development of one of the most spectacular expressions of Andean culture, the textiles of Paracas.

Paracas weavings embody the two basic thematic elements of pre-Colombian textile tradition; local tradition and custom together with astronomical influences. Intricate designs of animalistic, supernatural and human forms were embroidered on to dark backgrounds producing an exquisite effect. Knowledge of dyes was very advanced, and a total of 197 difference colours have been found. It was also a period of great technical innovation. All weaving techniques subsequently employed by pre-Colombian weavers appear in this era. The techniques included warp and weft stripe tapestry, brocade, double cloth and lace.

The site of Paracas, southern coastal Peru.

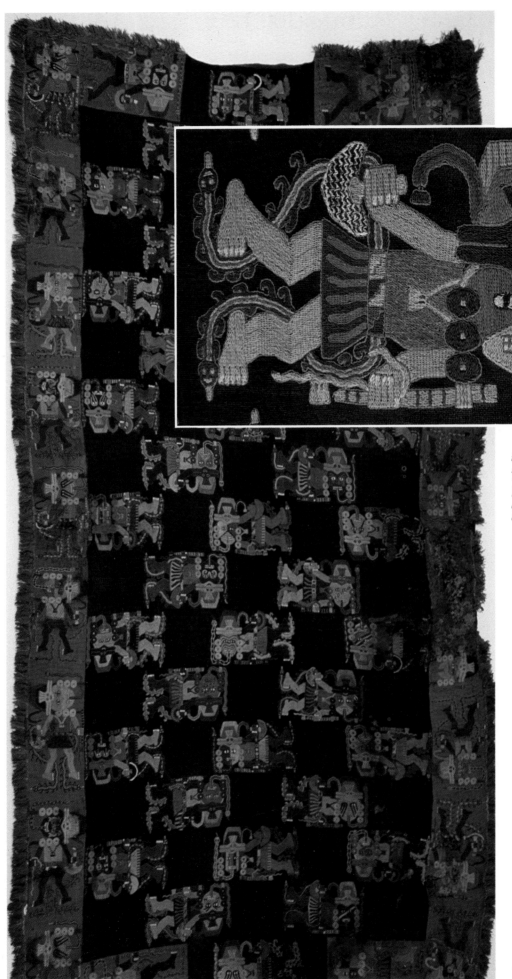

*Paracas woollen embroidery
in stem stitch. The design is a
series of highly decorative
'personajes' (note the trophy
heads on either side) each with
a Tumi in one hand and a long
arrow in the other.*

Chancay Culture (100 B.C. - 1200 A.D.)

In the valleys of Chancay, in the central coastal region, a great variety of sophisticated textiles have been discovered; brocades, embroidered weavings, exquisite gauze, cloth adorned with finely worked feathers and metal objects, and notably a great number of painted and printed cloths. Designs are typically geometric and reticulated, with much use of parallel lines and chequered patterns, and black-line geometric form on a white background is a distinctive Chancay style.

White and brown cotton cloth was common and often painted. The textiles show elaborate trimmings, and borders for which coloured wool was used, and fringes of single or multi-colour are a characteristic feature. Another distinctive find from this period are the small embroidered cloth dolls found with the burials. Whereas anthropomorphic figures are typical of the designs of Paracas, graceful fish and sea-bird forms predominate and a simple elegance characterises Chancay designs.

A Chancay burial ground, central coastal Peru.

*Natural white cotton cloth painted with
reddish brown sea-bird design, a Chancay
grave-doll and Tapestry with cotton warp and
wool weft, and a slit-warp fringe with bird design.*

Inca and post-Inca Period (1300 A.D. onwards)

Sadly, very few weavings from this period have survived, and of those most have deteriorated badly as a result of the climatic conditions of the mountainous regions. Research into the textiles of this period is limited, and the serious lack of textiles makes dating and identification extremely difficult. Occasionally one is lucky to find an old person who has inherited a piece of cloth from several generations back, but while this can be important it is not always reliable.

The Incas employed the weaving techniques developed by their predecessors, but worked in a much more decorative style, exploiting the expressive potential of colour. By the time the conquistadors arrived, weaving had reached such heights of technical and artistic achievement that they were astounded at its splendour. Spanish colonisation widely affected textile production in the Andean region as it did throughout the New World. Despite the erosion of traditional community structures, however, and the coercion of the indigenous population to work the mines and meet tribute obligations, weaving continued, and the treadle loom and new fibres brought from Europe were incorporated into textile production as were elements of European religious design.

A 16th Century drawing by Guaman Poma de Ayala showing Spanish authority over the native weavers.

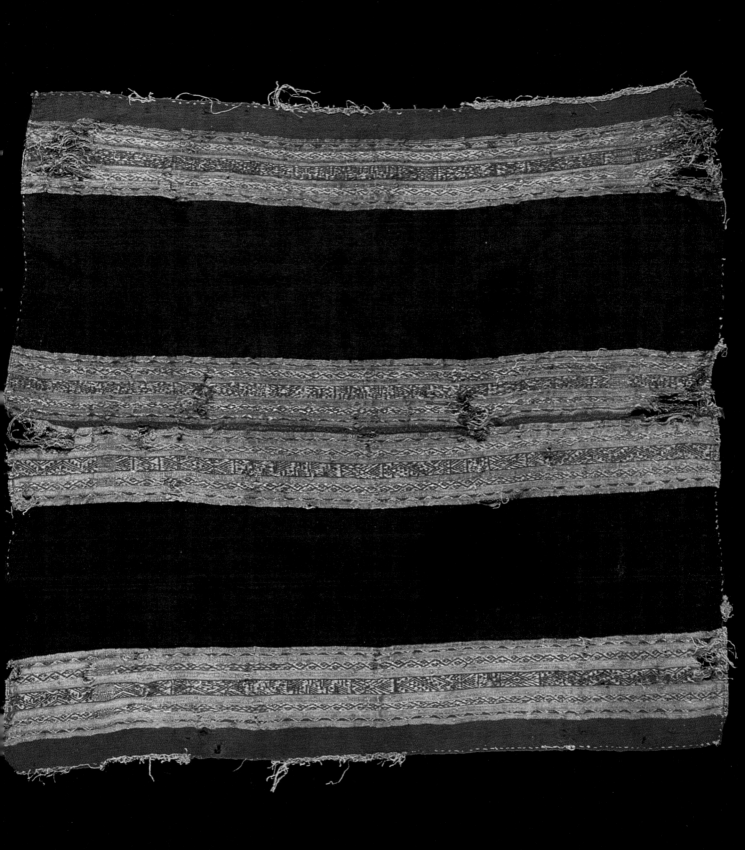

Two pieces of warp-faced alpaca cloth with silver threads in the brocade sewn together down the centre to form what is believed to be a 'Lliclla'. (Size: warp 95cm, weft 85cm)

Fibres

The basic materials of the pre-Colombian weavers were brown and white cottons, and the glossy hair or 'wool' of the llama and domesticated alpaca. The very fine silky hair of the wild vicuna, another cameloid was highly prized and also used, though to a much lesser extent. Occasionally human hair or reed was employed, and the Incas began to weave with gold and silver thread. The Spaniards introduced sheep's wool, silk, flax and metallic thread, which were readily adopted.

Nowadays synthetics such as acrylic, orlon and rayon have become widely available. Their comparative cheapness and labour-saving benefits mean that the traditional fibres, for all their textural superiority, are being disregarded more and more. Unfortunately this process, which only began in recent decades, threatens to severely undermine, if not destroy, literally milleniums of cultural tradition as knowledge and skill in the preparation and use of natural fibres is lost as family and social organisation adapts to meet today's economic requirements.

Spinning

The ancient Peruvians twisted yarn by hand, without the aid of a spindle or spinning wheel. The introduction of the drop spindle helped speed up this lengthy process but it was still a slow activity. The pre-Colombian weavers nevertheless became highly skilled spinners and produced some of the finest spun cloth in the world (over 100 threads per square cm have been counted in one sample of antique cloth). They learned to vary the spinning process according to the function of the desired cloth, producing single thread yarn, or twisting or spinning together several fine threads to vary colour and quality.

Ayacucho women using a drop-spindle.

The drop spindle is still widely used in rural areas today. The raw wool, after washing, goes through a number of stages. Initially a small spindle draws out a single strand, then a larger spindle is employed to combine two single strands to form a 2-ply yarn. A third spinning makes the yarn twist back on itself. In this way different coloured yarns can be used to produce varying shades of colour.

The spinning wheel, like the treadle loom, was introduced by the Spanish, but its use was not adopted in all parts, the campesinos preferring the mobility permitted by their traditional equipment. Weaving then, as now, was not always a primary occupation of the Indian community, priority being given to agriculture. Spinning and weaving would be set aside during the months of preparation of the land, seeding and harvesting. When harvesting was over, the Indian woman would carry her spindle and collapsible back-strap loom to the grazing land to watch over her sheep and alpaca, and produce cloth for personal use. Those communities that relied more upon production of textiles than agriculture more readily adopted the wheel and treadle loom, often combining use of old and new tools.

Interestingly enough the Peruvians, when using the drop spindle do not always spin clockwise. Anti-clockwise spinning is sometimes used for yarn to finish the edges of their cloth as it is believed to bring good luck and remove evil spirits. This type of spinning (Z) is called *lloqe*.

A woman of San Pedro de Cajas at her spinning wheel.

Looms

From pre-Colombian times to the present day, the back-strap loom and the horizontal loom have been the most widely used in Peru. The horizontal loom consists of two parallel pieces of wood pegged out by four stakes driven into the ground, *chauro,* with the warp threads stretched out between the two bars, *kakinas.*

Back-strap looms are used for more delicate pieces of work (finely woven belts, headbands). This can be carried around by the weaver, one end being attached by a cord to a tree or post, while the other end is held by a strap passing around the lower back of the weaver who then controls the warp tension by moving forwards or backwards. The entire warp is thus exposed, and flexible, which limits the length of the cloth. The width is determined by the hand to hand passage of the bobbin carrying the weft and is normally some 60 to 80 cm. When a wider fabric is required two pieces are sewn together lengthways.

With the introduction of the European treadle loom in the 16th century the problem of length was overcome, and the greater manoeuvreability afforded to the body meant that width could also be increased. This loom is widely used in Peru, and particularly around Lake Titicaca where a plain wool cloth called *bayeta* is produced for shirts and skirts and traditional short legged trousers. In recent years the treadle loom has been used to produce a variety of other articles for trade. Ayacucho has become famous for its rugs and wall hangings, while villages around Huancayo in Central Peru weave very beautiful alpaca textiles.

Vertical looms such as those used in Asian countries also appear to have been used during pre-Colombian times, as large textiles of several metres' width have been found dating from this period. There is evidence of this kind of loom today in villages around Cajamarca in northern-central Peru, and recently simple vertical looms have appeared in the town of Ayacucho, in the central Andean area.

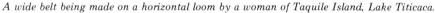

A wide belt being made on a horizontal loom by a woman of Taquile Island, Lake Titicaca.

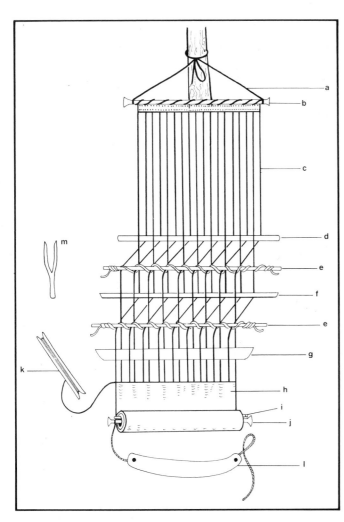

The structure of the back-strap loom.

a. *Awatanka* Small cords used to attach the upper loom bar to a given position.

b. *Kakina* Warp beam.

c. *Pampan* Warp threads.

d. *Tokoroq* Coarse rod separating the two warp sections.

e. *Kallwa* The heddle rods of the loom which vary according to the complexity of the cloth.

f. A small baton.

g. *Minekumay* Weft beater.

h. Woven cloth or web.

i. Rolling stick.

j. *Kakinas* Lower warp beam.

k. Shuttle and weft thread.

l. *Wakaqara* Strap passed around the lower part of the weaver.

m. *Ruki* A small beater that the weaver has in is hand. Can be of wood or bone.

Above: *The horizontal loom used in Juli in the Lake Titicaca region.*

Left: *A man of Taquile using the treadle loom to weave 'Bayeta'.*

Right: *A woman of Paccaritampo near Cusco using the back-strap loom.*

Natural Dyes

Pigments from animal, plant and mineral sources have been used from ancient times (3000 B.C.) onwards. The earliest weavings bear witness to the extensive range of colours known to the ancient Peruvians, although some of the materials and dyeing techniques employed are not now understood.

Much of our present knowledge stems from the time of the Incas whose tongue, Quechua, is one of the official languages of contemporary Peru. The extent and importance of dyeing skills can be judged by the elaborate Quechua terminology for the processes or *tallunduni* involved. Dyeing was complex and time-consuming, requiring considerable skills and an intimate knowledge of plant life. The Incas were able to produce colours of many shades, both bright and subdued which neither faded nor 'bled'.

Since the latter part of the 19th century the use of traditional methods has steadily declined as aniline dyes from Europe have been utilised. The aniline dyes are relatively cheap, widely available and require little preparation. However, the last two decades have seen the growth of a demand for 'natural dyed' textiles and this has helped to revive, in places, an inheritance that was rapidly disappearing.

To do justice to the complex work of the Andean dyers would take many more pages of explanation than can be included here, so I shall say merely a few words about the sources of various important dyes and mordants in use today.

The table below details some of the more commonly used plants.

Commonly used Natural Dyes

DYE SOURCE			PART USED	COLOUR
Native name	Botanical name	English name		
ALISO	*alnus jorullensis*	type of alder	leaves	yellows/greens
ANTACO	*rebulnium celiatum*	—	roots	greens
AYRAMPU	*Berberis sp.*	barberry	fruit	blue
CASARA de CEBOLLA	*callium sativum*	onion	skin	yellow
CHAPI	*gallium*	bedstraw		reds/browns
COCHINILLA	*coccus cacti*	cochineal		pinks/reds/blacks
EUCALIPTO	*eucaliptus globulus*	eucalyptus	leaves	gold/browns
HIERBA SANTA	*cestrum hediodinum*	—	fruit	blue
INDIGO	*indigofera Anil L.*	—	leaves	blue
LENGUA de VACA	*rumex crispis*	curled dock	plant	green
LIQUENES	*rocella, parmelia sp.*	lichen	plant	yellows/browns
MOLLE		elderberry	fruit	yellows/greens
NOGAL	*juglans neotropica*	—	bark, leaves, fruit	yellows/golds/browns
PACHAMARCA	*bidens andicola*	type of marigold	leaves	orange
PULALOJO	*rumex acetellosa*	sheeps sorrel	plant	green
QUINUAL	*polylepsis incana*	—	leaves, bark	beige
SALVIA	*salvia sagitata*	sage	leaves	yellow
TARA	*caesalpina tinctoria*	—	seed pods	browns/greys

The cochineal insect that lives on the leaves of the nopal cactus provides the principal dye. The history of its use is unclear and it is uncertain whether the insect was bred in coastal areas, as done in Mexico, or in the lower Andean basin. Cochineal dye was used by the pre-Colombian weavers who obtained various colours ranging from red, through purple to black. It is interesting to note that the villages around Cajamarca still dye fabrics black with the aid of cochineal, whereas in Hualhuas near Huancayo various shades of red are produced from it.

Vegetable dyes are procured from various sources: leaves, fruits and seeds of various shrubs and flowers, lichen, tree bark and roots. Traditional mordants are still employed to fix the colours and these include alum, human urine, salt, ash and lime juice. The choice of dyes and mordants depends partly on availability of materials and partly on local tradition. Some mordants are valued also for their colouring properties. In San Pedro de Cajas human urine is widely used as a fixing agent and also to provide a soft yellow. In villages near Huancayo and Ayacucho a mordant is produced by mixing urine with plant extracts.

There are several hundred plants used in different localities and most plants will render some colour. Potatoes, corns, eucalyptus leaves, onion skin and holly-tree berries are but a few of the commonest.

Above: *'Cochineal' living on cactus.*

Right: *A 16th Century drawing by Guaman Poma de Ayala showing a girl picking herbs.*

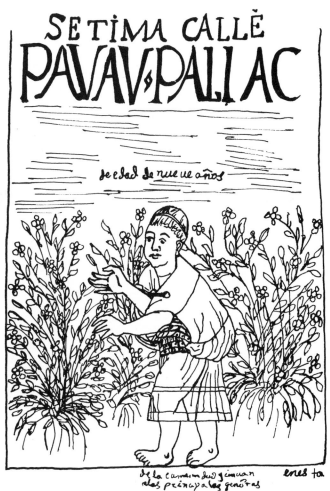

Symbolism

The use of symbolism was very important to the Andean civilisations. In pre-Colombian times, no system of writing was developed, instead various visual communicative systems evolved using different mediums to record and transmit information of social significance. Symbolism abounds in the highly figurative designs woven for special articles of clothing, such as *ponchos, mantas (llikllas)* and *chumpis,* which have been responsible for perpetuating a wealth of symbols. But before we look more closely at the symbolism used in weaving it is important to note the other communicative systems employed. Stones were traditionally engraved with figures thought to have magical properties, which related to constellar activity, and may have been used in astronomical predictions and some of the symbols occur in weaving. A system of ideograms was devised following the Spanish conquest for recording on paper Catholic prayers. But most important was the *quipu,* a system introduced by the Incas for recording mathematical data.

The *quipu* consisted of a series of knots on a string, each knot possessing a numerical value. From the evidence available it appears that the visual symbols used in weaving could vary in meaning from community to community. The Incas, however, imposed their *quipu* as a standard and unifying system throughout their empire, and it became the basic tool of social administration. It is interesting to note that William Burns Glyn, a researcher who spent many years investigating the *quipu,* has claimed that a correlation exists between symbols occuring in weaving and the values of *quipu* knots. He believes that the Incas had the potential to translate the information of the *quipu* into the graphic symbolism of weavings.

In the weavings the motifs commonly employed have been used to symbolise all that is of vital importance to the community: its magical and religious obligations, festival times and constellation movements. The weaver did not express personal life in the garment but was concerned with matters of tradition, to reflect the repetition in life. Then, as now, innovation was not a primary concern, although use of colour and design layout were forms of personal expression.

Not every motif has symbolic significance. Senora Gertrud Solari who has spent many years in very able research into the symbolism has found that many figures were woven in simply to isolate different motifs or group several motifs together. Most are symbolic however, although the weavers' knowledge of them varies. In some cases both weaver and wearer know the origins of the design motifs. Others know only the names and when questioned as to why these motifs have been worked will reply, as so often happens, "We have always done it".

With the arrival of the Spanish in the 16th century a new era of symbolism commenced as elements of Catholicism were incorporated and old and new designs appeared side by side. Mystical symbols such as *inti* (the sun) or *pacha-mama* (mother earth) may be found beside a horse figure. The execution of Tupac Amaru, who led the last Indian revolt against the Spanish, is represented in a motif commonly found in *mantas* of the Sacred Valley of the Incas, near Cusco. The motif symbolises Tupac Amaru being pulled apart by four horses of Pizarro's guards, which reportedly took place in Cusco's Plaza de Armas.

Sometimes confusion has arisen as original significance has become mixed with, or superceded by, a new meaning. The cross symbol is an obvious example. In pre-

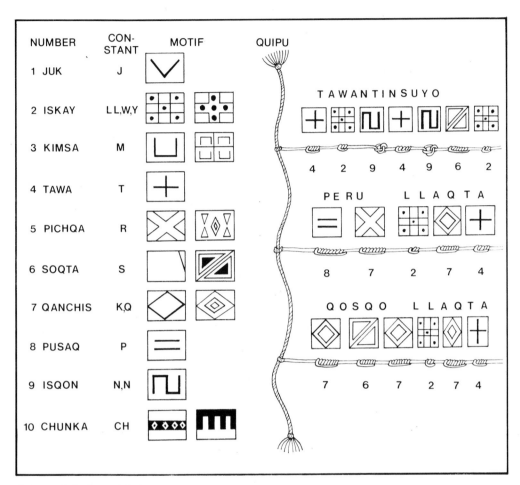

Quipu and the Inca alphabet.

William Burns Glyn, using computers, claims that the Incas could communicate through motif representation on ceramics and woven cloth, and could transfer information from a quipu to these other objects and vice versa.

Hispanic times the cross had varying significance. It was the symbol of a major festival, the *Fiesta del Cruz* which takes place with much dancing, drinking and music, on 3rd May each year, and was originally to celebrate the appearance of a constellation thought to herald the season of dry weather. Another example is the *Cruz de la Siembra* or guardian of the field, the significance of which has been eclipsed by the Christian cross.

Symbolism and meaning in Andean culture is a complex area and largely unexplored. Señora Solari has made inroads in her studies of various articles of clothing and these provide us with a detailed and illuminating analysis of certain motifs. The following symbols, extracted from her previously unpublished work identify some of the motifs which are used repeatedly in Andean textiles.

Symbolic Designs and Ideograms

In order to give an idea of the world of the Andean Indian, some examples of figures and patterns from different Andean regions with a short description of their symbolism are given.

All figures and designs are variable, depending on what the weaver wishes to express and are formed by the arrangement of coloured threads. Since before the Spanish conquest up to today it is the women who have woven textiles with symbolic designs. These are mainly belts, shoulder cloths, ponchos, coca bags, and small cloths *huachalas* used to wrap the offerings to the deities or for other festive uses.

Some of these woven figures and designs are also to be found in ceramics, stone work and jewellery.

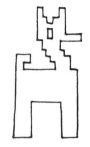

Llama

The *llama* not only plays an important role in the daily life of the Indian but is also thought to be the companion of the dead into the next world. It is worshipped and venerated in a constellation in which it plays the role of protector of llamas, alpacas and flocks of sheep.

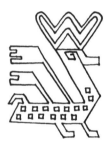

Taruka

The mountain deer belongs to the holy mountain *Auquis* and is believed to be the animal which carries the treasures of the mountain gods and spirits. The deer is revered as an *Auqui* or deity of the third grade. Its image is also found among offerings to the deities.

Ñuñuma — 'Duck'

This is the symbol for 'Mother of the Water'. The Quechua word is made up of 'nunu' (breast) and 'uma' (main, leader). In the Aymara language 'uma' means water. In the pre-Spanish days, according to information obtained from the island of Taquile, this sign was connected with *Viracocha* and was used to represent this diety.

Pata - Chakuna — 'Ducks in disorder — ducks in commotion'

The local Indians explain *Chakuna* as the wild, frantic flight of the birds while preparing their nests or while being hunted. Synonyms in Quechua and Aymara mean, stones lying on the path (even nowadays stones for use in sacrifice are picked up from the path), indivisable, detached, damp, originating from dampness (suggesting fertility).

Chiwaku — 'Black bird'

This bird is connected in legend with abundance and harvest. It 'sows' potatoes in October and from that moment on does not sing again till he 'tastes his harvest' in April. In the rainy season his rump is damp, in the dry season, dry. It is a good sign when the *Chiwaku* is present at the sacrifice rituals. Synonyms in Quechua and Aymara mean, among other things, sexual union, selection of the seeds, future creation of things.

Jesa Champi Urpi — 'Doves' nest made out of triangular axe blades'

Urpi, (dove) is the symbol for matrimonial union. In the legends the lovers were changed into doves, who then created life—important things for humanity (springs, etc). The word *'champi'*, a metal instrument for work and war, also means 'large mushroom' (mushrooms were used in secret rites). If one cuts a mushroom vertically one obtains the form of an axe and of a woman's sexual organs.

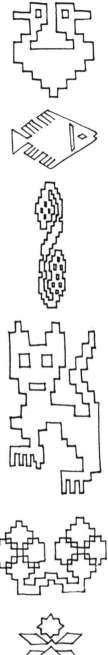

Pescado — 'Fish'

This is considered as the holy god 'Viracocha'. Viracocha himself is supposed to have put the fish into water for the use of mankind.

Culebra de Dos Cabezas — 'Snake with two heads'

The tail of this type of snake looks similar to the head. They live under the earth and are only visible in pure spring water. The legendary two-headed snake was the deity *Amaru*, which, defeated in battle by another deity, turned itself into stone. Even now the inhabitants scratch powder from stone and consume it in order to be protected from illness. The snake is also a fertility symbol and is used in magic cults and ceremonies.

Puma — 'Puma'

The *puma* is regarded as the god of the *punas* (high plains of the Andes). It is also called *Aija* (meat, sex organ). *Aija* literally means 'distributor of foodstuffs', 'giver of something to everybody'. The image of the *puma* is sometimes found on roofs as a protector of family fortune.

Waita Ticca — 'Flower'

Flowers are nearly always found amongst the offerings to the cosmic deities. They belong to the holy beings of nature whose power can heal, protect, or purify sinners. Girls adorn themselves with flowers in order to show that they are ready for marriage. Personal flower adornments show hierarchy during festivities. *Waita* also means 'feather'. This is not only a sign of status but can also be used in offerings or marriage ceremonies.

Casca-lucero — 'The morning and evening star—Venus'

This star is holy and even now highly revered. Rites performed in its honour commence at Whitsun. The farmer follows its path in the sky which tells him when to sow the different crops. Spiritual authorities of the community recognise the different phases of the planet forecasting the natural phenomena for the coming year. We find connections with 'symbols of hierarchy', 'princess', 'white', 'to cloud over' in the various synonyms of the Quechua word for Venus.

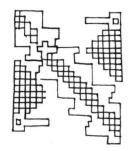

Kenko-Mayu — 'Meandering river in zig-zag'

An identical design is to be found in pre-Inca textiles. The word *Kenko* is interpreted as 'something from the olden days', 'holy', 'forbidden', 'to throw oneself with effort onto something', 'precipitously'.

Kocha or Jocha — 'Lake, pond, spring'

This sign is connected with places of water. Sacrifices are made to it and sins are cleaned with its water (*Jocha*—sins). The springs that have sources on the surface are shown as the 'eyes of mother earth'. The ceremony for the cult of water is celebrated in September. *Jocha* has a second meaning—the aura of the sun and moon.

Alpaka

This sign is not connected with the animal alpaca. The word's original form is ALPA-PACA. *Alpa* means 'earth', 'usable fields'; *Paka* means 'secret', 'hidden mystery', hence the origin of its magic context. We find the following meanings in its synonyms: 'chewing of coca leaves'; 'to plough', 'eagle', 'mushroom', 'fungi', 'shot'. If the X appears without the rectangular border it shows the Andean Indians' obligation to make sacrifices.

Sojta Suyu

'*Sojta*' means six; '*Suyu*' means lands. The six 'lands' signify the lands of common ownership in an Indian community. Since times past each inhabitant has had his plot, the size of which varies according to wealth and hierarchy.

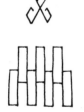

Kancha de Papa con Bandera

Kancha—'fields fenced for a special purpose' eg for the use of and in honour of the village holy man, a feast in whose honour is nearly always connected with pre-Conquest festivity. *Papa*—potato. The potato is a holy, blessed vegetable. *Bandera* —Unancha (Quechua)—'sign of honour'. Since pre-Spanish days everything successful, whether harvest or festivity is honoured with a flag.

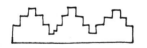

Orjos — 'Mountain'

The highest peak which dominates a region plays an important role in mythology and is thought to be the habitat of the ancestors, the highest deity of the region known as *wamani* or *Auqui*. Mountains are also considered as living beings to whom one has to sacrifice.

Cuenta de Meses

The months are counted by the number of times the threads are woven from above to below. This shows in which month the cloth was woven.

Calvary Cross

This cross has many meanings. Some are connected with the church and some with pre-Christian rites. Crosses of flowers and grass made for the festivities, for rains to help seeds grow, are carried by local dignitaries to the springs and mountain lakes. The cross symbol also appears in ancient stone signs throughout Peruvian territory. The cross with the figure of Christ was used as a secret symbol for mother earth after the Spanish conquest.

Left: *A pre-columbian cross at a road junction.*

   Below: *A christian symbol at the pre-columbian 3rd of May Festival of the Cross.*

▲
◀ *The 3rd of May Festival of the Cross, Huancane, Lake Titicaca.*

Chumpis (Belts)

Chumpi is the Quechua word for 'belt'. Chumpis have traditionally played an important role in the lives of the Indians and continue to be used in the more traditional communities where they are hand-woven and often elaborately decorated. The belts are responsible, probably more than any other article of clothing, for the preservation of ancient motifs, a result of the Indians' belief in their magical properties. Chumpis are thought to have protective and purifying qualities and have been used as a medium for communicating with the gods. To this day some communities in the Cusco area place chumpis on sacred mountain tops, or *Auqui*, each chumpi bearing a particular ideogramic message for the gods.

Traditionally women will give birth lying on a chumpi, and the baby is wrapped in a *Walt'ana*, a soft chumpi which I have been told ensures that the child will grow properly. When the child suffers from an attack of *susto* (literally, fright) wild flowers are placed on the child's brow which is then wound round with a narrow chumpi. The type of chumpi worn may indicate social status and in some areas such as the island of Taquile in Lake Titicaca the distinctive local pattern makes the wearer's community immediately recognisable. In pre-Colombian times the dead were buried together with the family chumpi.

The women, from adolescence onwards, gird themselves with a chumpi which is worn under the skirt and sometimes amulets relating to secret lovers, or worn to deter undesired suitors, are attached to the chumpi. Women also wear *huatana*, small narrow belts plaited into the hair to show their marital status. During wedding festivals it is common for the bridegroom to 'lasso' the bride with a chumpi, and on the wedding night the matrimonial godparents traditionally cross the bridal bed with two chumpis.

While travelling recently in Peru, I had two experiences which help to illustrate the significance of the chumpi today. In the village of Paccarinambo in the highlands near Cusco I observed an old woman weeping at the grave of her husband while holding in her hand the chumpi he had worn. In a community near Lake Titicaca I was invited to cut a little girl's hair—the first time it had been cut—which is a traditional way to become the child's godfather. The girl's hair was then placed in a bag and fastened with the belt she had used during the early days of her childhood.

Opposite: *'Waltana' narrow belt from the village of Chinchero, Cusco Province.*

'Chumpi' long wide belt from the village of Challuahuacho, Apurimac Province.

'Chumpi' short wide belt from the highlands of Puno, Lake Titicaca.

A small purse from the Ccolquepta community, Cusco province.

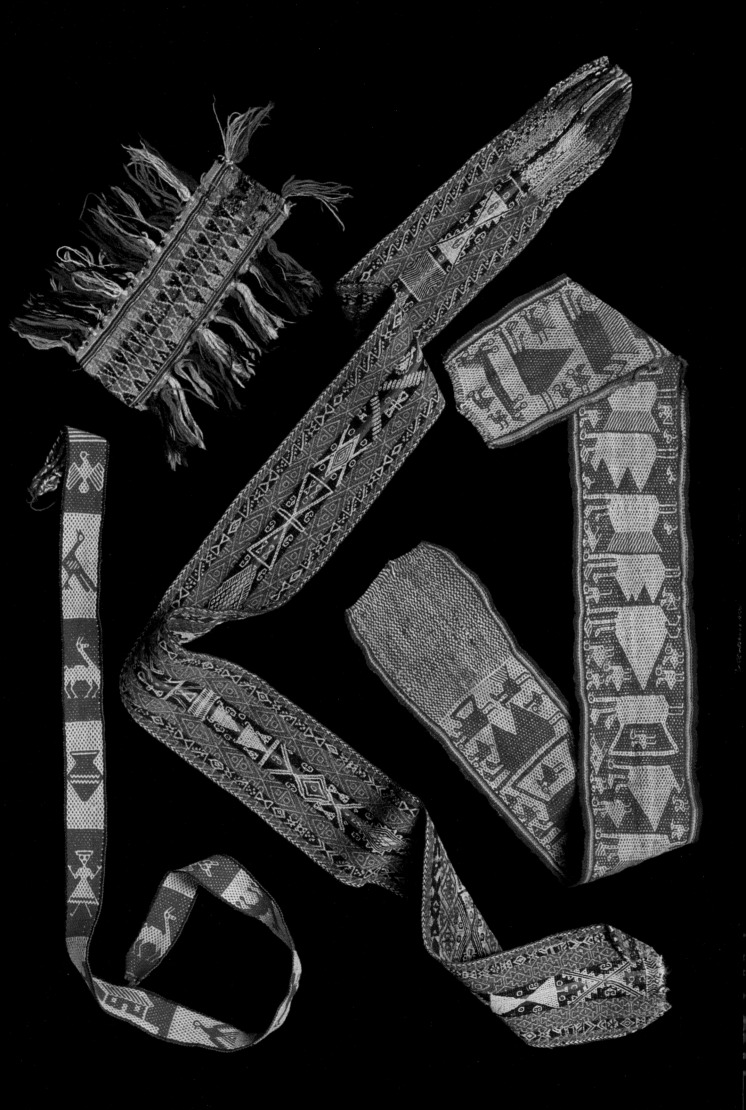

Chumpis and Symbolism:
Agricultural calendar woven on a Taquile belt

The last part of this section on chumpis looks at a belt woven on Taquile Island which is of particular interest because its design relates to the Islanders' agricultural calendar. The belt measures 90cm x 15cm. It is no longer worn but is thought to have been used during harvesting, and was lately woven especially to bring together various symbols known to the islanders from ages past. It is most likely that the calendar evolved during the Inca era because several of the symbols refer to Inca deities and much of the vocabulary used to describe each symbol is Quechua. The calendar is divided into twelve sections which may be coincidental, but suggests it has been influenced by the Gregorian calendar. Exactly how and why it evolved is not known but it nevertheless provides a fascinating cultural record of the lifestyle of a community living on a small island.

The symbols are derived from the agricultural cycles, the island's environment and from supernatural forces. The symbols basically show when certain events occur, but, more importantly, allude to the significance of these events or behavioural patterns in predicting the course of nature. What is more interesting is the belief that the material elements in the Islanders' environment could be used as omens for predicting what nature had in store. Hence the Islanders associated birds laying eggs in their nests with the good news that rain would follow, and large numbers of eggs meant a good harvest. If however the *Kate-Kate*, a small black bird, was seen flying in the wrong direction over a house, bad luck or death would follow.

The twelve symbols are included here with brief descriptions of their content and meaning. Each symbol contains a wealth of significant details which, unfortunately, it is not possible to analyse in depth here. But from an examination of the symbols one can suggest that the calendar was not concerned with cause and effect, but rather the realisation of behaviours which when observed could be interpreted to predict the future. The use of these patterns in their weavings shows the importance the Islanders give to the forces which are decisive in the pattern of life itself.

I have given the Quechua name for each symbol and where possible suggested an English interpretation of this. Finally I would stress that the interpretation of the calendar as a whole has no scientific root, and is merely the popular interpretation of the people of Taquile themselves which has passed down through generations.

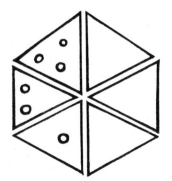

Musok Huata Kallary — 'The new month'

This period relates to the rotation of crops and is represented by a hexagram of six *suyos*, the six regions which historically divide Taquile. Three of these suyos are identified with dots which indicate that these will be ploughed to produce oca, potatoes and grain. The other sections which remain fallow.

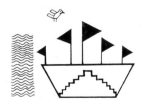

Ttecay Guella — 'The month of flowers'

This period is represented by a section of ploughed 'suyo', *chakmay*, a small bird, *Chinuaco* and a *Rosas altar*. The chakmay represents the readiness of the soil for cultivation. The rosas altar probably refers to the festival of the 'Virgin of Candelara'. The crying of the 'chinuaco' means a cold year ahead.

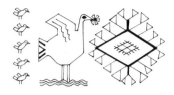

Jappman Pahuana Quilla

The third period is represented by a large bird with her off-spring. A large number of off-spring indicates a fruitful year ahead, and a small number a poor harvest. It is further believed that if the off-spring walk ahead of the mother, an early harvest is to be expected and if they walk behind, the harvest will be late.

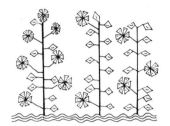

Chacra Athapey Quilla — 'The month of reaping the fruits of labour'

The fourth period is represented by three plants in flower: the potato, the oca and, possibly, the broad bean. If during this period the plants are in flower then an early frost is forecast. Hailstorms are predicted by the flights of birds and their behaviour patterns. If birds are seen sitting on the flowers and looking downwards towards the earth then a bad harvest and hunger is predicted.

Hatun Cusecuy Huakaicha Quilla — 'The month of paying Pachamama, the mother earth'

The fifth period is represented by a symbol similar to that of the second period. A 'rosas altar' represents the festival of 3rd May, 'Fiesta del Cruz'. All marriages take place on this date. The festival celebrating the birth of Taquile also takes place in this period.

Cuska Huata Cusecuy — 'The half year'

The sixth period is represented by a house or *wasi* which may represent the end of the harvest with stacks of produce in the house. The sign *chuño* on the right, may represent the Inca festival of 'inti Raymi', held on 24th June. It is in this period that *chuño*, the dried potatoes, are prepared.

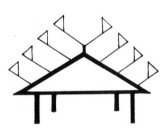

Jallpa Tejray Quilla

This period is represented by *altar wasi*, which is similar to the 2nd and 5th periods. From observations, the 'altar' sign always represents some sort of festival and in this case probably represents the festival of Santiago of Taquile. All agricultural activities have ended and fishing and weaving begin.

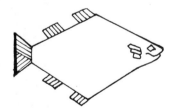

Huata Jhahuana Quilla — 'The month to think of the whole year'

This month is represented by the *soche* fish. Here the fishes' behaviour would be used to forecast the coming year. If the eggs of the 'soche' are found in shallow waters, a dry year is expected. If they appear in deep water then much rain is expected.

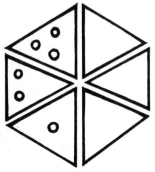

Sumak Ijuata — 'Better year'

The ninth period is represented by six 'suyos', as is the first period. The previous period of the fish symbol plays an important role in the ploughing pattern of the 'suyos' during the coming year. If the fish laid eggs in shallow water, then rotation of the crops follows the last year's pattern, if not the crop rotation is changed and other crops are seeded.

Huata Yupaskq Quilla

The tenth period is represented by the *Chaska*, a bright star with four smaller stars in its centre. It refers to the bright constellation seen in the north. To the left of this star is a symbol that represents land which is ploughed, and the dotted symbols refer to the suyos to be cultivated.

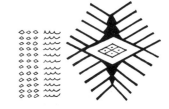
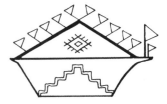

Paramanta Huakay Seloman

The symbol of the 11th period *mayo altar*, represented the festival of All Saints. If however the rainy season has not yet begun, sacrifices are made by going to the highest hill in the name of Pachamama. The symbol in the centre of the design is thought to represent mother earth.

Huata Tucuska Japperay Quilla — 'The month of hunger'

The last period is represented by a large bird with her off-spring in front and behind. If off-spring are observed following her and crying this forebodes hunger, because it is interpreted as the need to rear the stock before the next harvest can be gathered. If all the birds are observed in front of the mother bird, good fortune will follow.

Belt weaving on Taquile Island.

Taquile man with Wak'a loom.

Opposite: *Lake Titicaca seen from Taquile Island.*

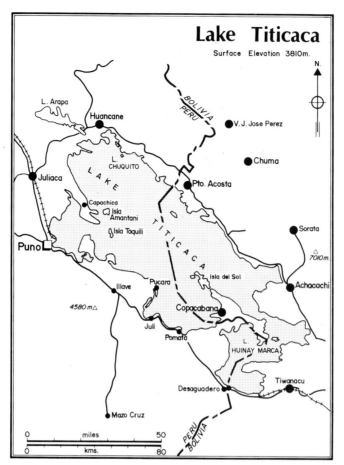

Lake Titicaca

Surface Elevation 3810m.

The Titicaca Basin

One of the most extraordinary textile traditions found in Peru belongs to the predominantly Aymara culture of the Lake Titicaca basin plateau. Lake Titicaca covers a vast area of some 81,300 square kilometres in the high mountains of South Eastern Peru, and at 3,820 metres (12,000ft) it is the highest navigable lake in the world. The area surrounding the lake has for 3,000 years been an important centre for textile production.

Aymara woman tending llamas near Lake Titicaca.

The first settlers of the region are thought to be the Urus Indians whose communities can still be seen on the small floating 'tortora' reed islands of the lake. With no land to cultivate, these Indians survive on fish and waterfowl from the rivers. They fish from small reed boats (balsa) and live in small thatched reed huts of the type used by their ancestors. Their language 'Puquina' is not related to Aymara nor Quechua, though Quechua is spoken by them as a result of trade with the nearby town of Puno and other Indian islanders.

The great majority of Indians in the area around the lake are of Aymara origin. They live on fish and work small plots of land, and tend alpaca and sheep which are seen grazing together on the hills around the lake. Their culture has proved remarkably resistent over the centuries to external influence. The Incas failed to force their customs or Quechua upon them and the Spaniards, for all the destructiveness of their colonizing zeal in other parts of the Andes had a limited effect on their way of life. Spanish influence though is seen in local customs, music and festivities, largely as a result of the adoption of Catholicism. The treadle loom which was brought from Europe is widely used, but the traditional back-strap loom has survived through centuries and the treadle loom has been used to complement rather than substitute it.

Nowadays however, the resistance to change brought from outside is fast crumbling. In recent years knitting has been introduced, and today more time is devoted to it than to weaving. The latter is done mostly for personal use. Markets have been found at home and abroad for the knitwear. The ancient traditions are in jeopardy from modernisation in the form of man-made fibres, and machinery introduced by the multi-national companies, and the increasing number of other self-interest groups. A skirt made of synthetic material can cost up to three times as much as the home product, but because of its novelty value the Indians often prefer to sell or barter their own products. The danger is, of course, that before they come again to find the beauty of their traditional skills, it may be too late to remember how a piece of cloth was made on a simple loom.

A floating island or 'Uru' on Lake Titicaca.

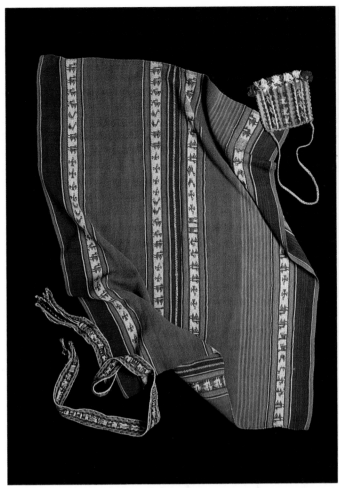

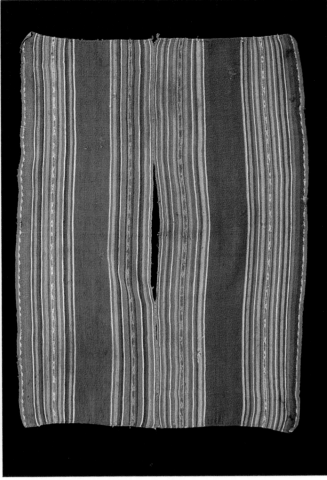

'Manta', 'Chumpi' and 'Chuspa' from Puno.

Man's small ceremonial poncho from Huancane, Lake Titicaca.

Striped grey manta and brown, red and blue manta with Puma footprint symbols, Lake Titicaca.

Taquile Island

If Lake Titicaca is the centre of the Andean world then Taquile must be the heart of it. Taquile lies gracefully in the centre of the lake, to the east of the peninsula of Capachina and Chucuito, and to the south of the island of Amantani. It is small and measures some four kilometres in length, and two kilometres in width, and its population of 1,300 is growing.

Taquile was highly prized by the Incas and when it became part of their empire its Aymara-speaking people had to adopt Quechua, and likewise the Inca sun-god *Inti* became their highest deity, and *Viracocha* was worshipped as the 'creator'. Under the Incas the island was divided into two *ayllus* or sections: *Uray ayllu* and *Hanaq ayllu*. Each ayllu was then subdivided into three *suyos*.

Today the traditional divisions continue and the *suyos* are ruled over by the same six families that have done so for centuries. A variety of crops are grown in each suyo: *oca*, a long, coloured potato; *abas*, broad beans; *papas*, potatoes; *Maiz*, corn; *trigo*, wheat; *quinua*, a grain rich in protein and a traditional food of the Incas. During the coldest months from June to August the potatoes are frozen and dried to make *chuño*. Fish is eaten, fresh and dried, as a regular part of the diet.

A boat or 'balsa' of tortora reeds, Lake Titicaca.

Above and following page: *Dancing on Taquile Island during the February Festival.*

Folk dances, music and the islanders' beautiful costume tradition have all survived the passage of time well, and pre-Colombian festivities are still celebrated. Even today sacrifices are made to the old deities, and it is fascinating to see the traditional customs associated with the sacred coca leaf (thought to be a gift from the gods), and *chicha,* a fermented corn juice as it is poured to the ground in the name of *Pachamama,* the mother earth, before it is drunk.

The costumes of the islanders are very colourful, and are made up of numerous articles of clothing each with its own name and significance. Families possess at least four different types of costume: for work, leisure, weddings and festivals. The daily costume is as colourful, if not as elaborate, as those for special occasions, and may be changed twice during the day.

All marriages take place on 3rd May, at the time that *Hatuni Chaska*, or Venus, appears in alignment with three other stars to form the Cruz del Sur. The marriage ceremony takes a week of preparation and three days and three nights of celebration with non-stop music, dancing, drinking of chicha and chewing of coca leaves. The *padrino,* or best man, is carefully chosen by the bridegroom's father and is responsible for the supply of coca leaves and chicha. In exchange the bridegroom must help the padrino in preparing his land and harvesting for a period of at least two years.

During the wedding ceremony the bride and bridegroom are tied together by their hands, the bride sitting apart from her husband-to-be, and below him. Only the padrino may feed the bridegroom. The bridegroom wears a red poncho provided by the padrino, which is passed down through generations. As a single man the bridegroom wears a hat that is half red and half white, and now for the first time he wears the *pinta-chullo*, a long red hat that shows he is married. He also wears a wedding *faja*, a wide red belt, and special sandals *qjojta*. His *chuspa* or coca bag is filled with coca leaves.

The bride sits elegantly in her wide *montera* hat, and her fastened hands are covered by a small cloth, a *Katana-oncoma*. A *quincha*, a small white cloth symbolising purity, is hidden in her skirt. She wears a wedding blouse or *gonna* and her skirt or *pollera* is made up of some twenty different layers of brightly coloured cloth. She too wears a faja and a black manta, known as a *chukoo*, completes her costume.

During the dancing the young men and women choose their partners for the coming year's wedding. Everytime a member of the family enters the wedding feast, coca leaves are exchanged and chicha is poured to the ground in the name of Pachamama. The bride and bridegroom sit bound together by their hands, and while the dancing and festivity continues around them, they must remain still for three days.

Cusco and the Sacred Valley of the Incas

There are two mystical legends relating to the foundation of the Inca empire. According to the first legend, Manco Capac left Lake Titicaca with his sister and his wife, Mama Ocllo, with a message from the Sun God, Inti, to found a city for the civilisation of mankind. With him, Manco Capac carried a sceptre which he lost in Lake Huamacaure, and it was here that he decided to build the city of Cusco. The second legend tells of Ayar Manco, Ayar Cachi, Ayar Uchu and Ayar Auco who left the cave of Tamputoco, and, in the company of their wives, set out on a journey on which they met with many adventures. All but Ayar Manco met with fateful ends, and so it fell to him to found the Inca empire. Whatever the interpretation given to these and other legends, it is a fact that the Incas came from a different region and settled in the area that is now Cusco. Here they founded a city that was to become the centre of their empire, Tawantinsuyo.

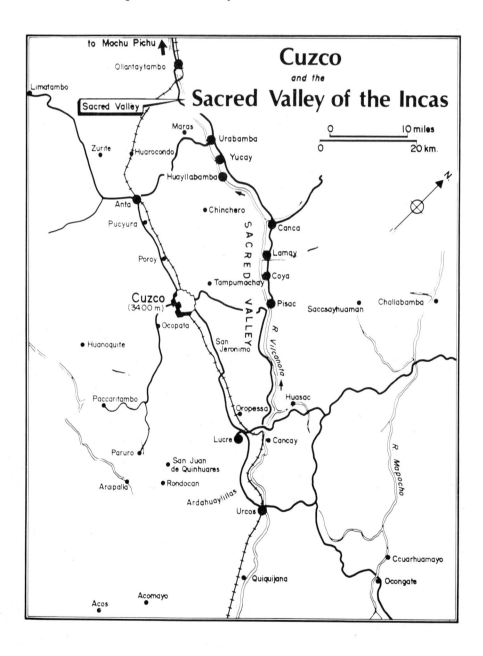

Cusco lies high in the Andes of south-eastern Peru, at an altitude of 3,400 metres, surrounded by snow-capped mountains and at the confluence of three rivers: the Tulumayo, the Huatamay and the Chunchulmayo. "Cusco was destined by nature", writes R. Porras, "to serve as a warm nest for a culture, a crossing of roads, a crucible of peoples, an Indian acropolis and a quadrant of solar history."

Today the Department of Cusco covers a varied geographical area taking in the basin plateau of Lake Titicaca to the north, the high Andean peaks and the Vilcanota river, whose waters flow through the fertile valley of Urubamba, known as the sacred valley of the Incas. This valley lies close to Cusco, and was well populated by the Incas. From this heartland the Incas rapidly conquered a vast area which extended the length of the Andes and the Pacific coast from northern Ecuador to central Chile.

Textiles were of utmost importance to the Incas, and much time and energy was devoted to their production. They were an important part of religious and marriage ceremonies and of burials, when the dead were interred in large black cloths and with other textiles. Large quantities of the finest textiles were woven specifically to be buried as ritual offerings, a custom that continued well after the arrival of the Spanish. The Conquistadors were astonished to find warehouses containing huge quantities of textiles, much of which, it is reported, was burned by the Incas to prevent its desecration by the Spanish. Moreover, the Incas regarded the art of weaving so highly that textiles even had their own deity, Aksu Mama, to whom weavings were sacrificed each year.

The Incas introduced the 'mita' which was a system of labour service and a form of taxation. Weaving was fundamental to their economy, and together with agriculture formed the basis for state revenue. Special cloth, known as 'cumbi', was woven for the Inca by specialist male weavers or 'qumpikamaqoq' to meet their labour obligations. Permanent settlements of 'qumpikamaqoq' were established and a large, comprehensive Quechua vocabulary evolved.

Below left: *Sunday Market, Pisac, Indians in processional costume; a custom surviving from Inca times.*

Below right: *A Chinchero woman visiting Cusco.*

'Cumbi' employed the tapestry weaving technique traditional to the Aymara culture. This culture had its centre at Tiahuanaco (Tiwanaku) south of Lake Titicaca, which from 600 - 1100 A.D. was the site of the first major highland civilisation. From here a distinctive artistic style spread throughout the Andes. Evidence of altiplano motifs are found in Inca mythology, and Aymara influence can be seen also in traditional Inca designs.

Tapestry weave emerged as the most prestigious weaving technique, and was reserved exclusively for use by Inca nobility. The ceremonial weavings of the Incas and early colonial period are among the most beautifully woven cloth ever produced. The warp-faced tradition was also important, though the complementary warp-weave technique was preferred. More complex designs could be worked on the horizontal loom, and this took priority over the back-strap loom. 'Chumpis', however, were typically woven on small back-strap looms, where the weaver fixed the warp to her toes, a method still seen around Cusco today. The treadle loom, however, was not widely adopted, and today is rarely seen in this region.

The Incas developed their own distinctive styles incorporating traditional designs and motifs. Their patterns are typically ordered and simple, often symmetrically arranged and with geometric forms. The best known Inca motif is the 'zig-zag with alternating eye' of the tapestry and warp-faced textiles. Other common motifs are the diamond pattern, representing 'Inti', and the double-headed snake, which, with the eight-point star 'Chaska' and the S-shaped motif, are still used today. Designs that were developed in the post-Inca period include the lizard and the frog, horses, human faces and the symbolic execution of Tupac Amaru (see section on symbolism).

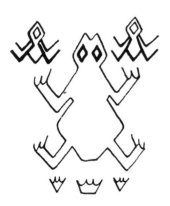

Right: *A 'Lliklla' from Huaca-Huaca in the Urubamba Valley. It contains both Inca and post-Inca symbols. 'Inkarri' their king was thought by the Incas to live beneath the earth. His expected reappearance is represented by frogs eggs found in damp earth at the edge of streams.*

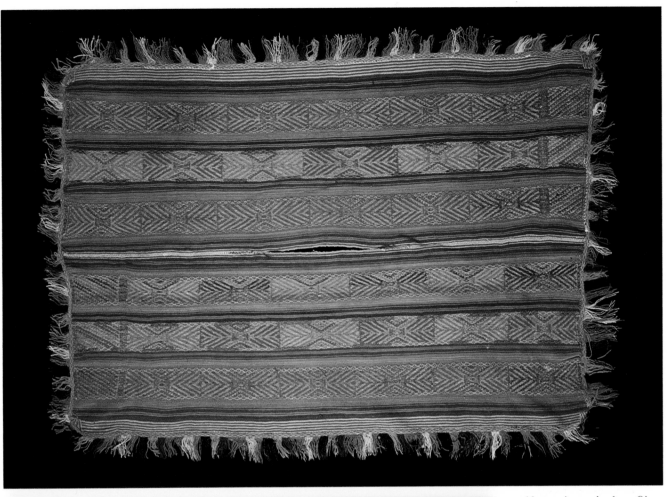

Above: *A poncho from Q'ero near Paucartambo. It contains symbols typifying the Cusco area and the sun god 'Inti'.*

A 'Lliclla' from Ocongate near Lauramarca. The silver pin 'Topo' is worn at the front.

A ceremonial poncho from Pisac in the Incas' sacred valley.

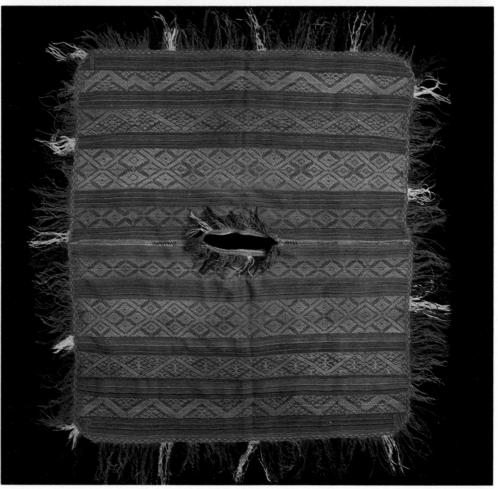

48

Previous page, top: *A girl from Pisac.*

Previous page, bottom left: *A small manta 'Unkhuña' and a small bag 'Chuspa'' both used to carry coca leaves.*

Previous page, bottom right: *Potatoes, beans, 'Chunos' and other small foods are eaten from different coloured small mantas called 'Unkhuñas'.*

Inca Costumes

The Spanish observed and documented the Incas' traditional costumes which were of great significance as were cloth articles in everyday use. Coca leaves were carried in a specially woven manta called an *Unkhuña* or a small bag, an *Acollina*. Mantas or *Chusi* were woven with simple shaped patterns for carrying potatoes or other agricultural products and the stripes were varied according to the product and whether it was for consumption in the house, sale in the market or storing seed.

Costumes were important indicators of social status in the local community. The Inca and his close relatives wore special costumes, which the Spanish quickly prohibited in order to eradicate the political symbol of the Inca. The Indians of both sexes wore tunic-like garments, and everyone wore some kind of distinguishing headgear. Later the Spanish passed laws to make Indian males adopt a style of clothing typical of the Spanish commoner, and in place of the 'Uncu' knee-length 'pantalones' were introduced, and short jackets called 'chapuetas'. The women also began to wear more European-style clothes, and the traditional 'Aksu' was replaced by a blouse 'blosa' and 'pollera' skirt. Headdress was restyled, and today many Indians still wear the 'montera' introduced by the Spanish. The shape and colours of the hats vary greatly according to locality. In Calca, in the sacred valley of the Incas, the Indians still wear large, round, red hats, and the Indians of Chachin and Choquecancha, which are neighbouring communities, wear small round hats of mixed colours.

Each community traditionally has its own costumes, and despite the social upheavals caused by the Spanish invasion, these traditions have continued up to this day. The conquest inevitably affected the native weaving tradition, though to a lesser degree in the remote highlands than on the coast. The Indians continued to use articles of native dress, and warp-faced weaving, the traditional technique used for common garments, survived in the highlands and inaccessible areas around Cusco. Inherited traditional colours and designs have carried down through past centuries so that today the uniformity of dress within a community provides its members with an identity and pride which in turn helps to maintain the cultural traditions in the face of strong external influence and rapid change.

Right: *The oldest couple in the 'sacred valley of the Incas' from the Amplay community near Pisac. Sadly the wife died in April, 1984, and the old man became broken and weak. Are we watching the death of a culture?*

Contemporary Weaving:
Ayacucho and San Pedro de Cajas

In order to evaluate the evolutionary development of Peruvian textiles I have ignored those communities where modern dyes and fibres have been introduced, but have chosen two areas, Ayacucho and San Pedro de Cajas, which have resisted these influences and have adapted themselves to the demands of the outside world.

In the Huancayo valleys, Cusco and the northern highlands, weaving is a secondary occupation and complementary to agricultural activities. However, in Ayacucho and San Pedro de Cajas it is looked upon as a primary source of income.

Throughout all these areas the treadle looms and spinning wheels have replaced the pre-Hispanic drop-spindle and back-strap loom providing greater efficiency and flexibility. Men and women work side by side to produce beautiful contemporary weavings. In Ayacucho the symbols used can be traced to pre-Colombian times and today the designs of the Paracas culture are still used on the rectangular rugs of naturally dyed sheep's wool.

In San Pedro de Cajas the designs have taken on a new dimension. Using the simplest technique the artist produces images of local scenery combined with abstract motifs. Here the unusual technique of wadding is used which involves introducing naturally dyed un-spun wool between the warp threads. The finished product appears more like a painting. Quite contrary to the traditional practice whereby all the members of the community express themselves using communal symbols, here, like the modern artist, each weaver expresses his or her own individuality and creative talent.

In Santa Anna, Ayacucho, the treadle loom has replaced the back-strap loom.

During recent years Ayacucho has been a centre of political unrest. Sadly the Indian population, mostly craft workers, have been leaving their ancestral land for the cities, mainly Lima, where they are far from the sources of material that they once used in their crafts. This has left Ayacucho with a handful of people facing an uncertain future.

Overpage: *Contemporary rugs with pre-columbian designs from Santa Anna, Ayacucho.*

A couple from the weaving community of San Pedro de Cajas.

The Uncertain Future

The pre-Colombian artistic expression which gave birth to some of the most valuable designs and techniques ever seen in the world is buried deep down in the sandy beaches of the Peruvian coastline. Today this region is inhabited by people of mixed European origin who have never understood or appreciated the spiritual and mystical aspects of Indian life.

The indigenous Indians have been forced to retreat to isolated valleys in the Andean highlands, but the temptations of materialism have meant that the European immigrants have introduced man-made fibres and aniline dyes to these valleys. In exchange, alpaca and llama fleece are exported to the western world leaving the Indians with little choice of material.

Today some communities have adapted themselves successfully to producing modern textiles using traditional techniques and materials. Others have succumbed to market forces and risk losing their artistic integrity and cultural heritage producing goods of artificially dyed, synthetic fibres. It seems ironic that the tradition of Indian weaving should have survived the Spanish invasion, even absorbing European methods, but now is besieged by the economic forces of the western world, and is in danger of annihilation.

The oldest inhabitant of Peru, about 130 years old.

▲ *A Calca couple.*

Supper. ▼

▲ *Responsibility.*

Harvest. ▼

▲ *Face to face.*

'Pacha Mama'. ▼

▲ 'Matè' charing.

A Shipibo, Amazona. ▼

A little girl from Pisac.
Will she be a back-strap weaver?

Glossary

ACOLLINA 'Coca' bag.

AKSU Rectangular cloth which women wear on the back, hanging from the belt or covering the entire back; a tunic-style dress during the Inca period.

AYMILLA Bayeta blouse.

BAYETA Woollen cloth.

CAITO Handspun yarn.

CHUMPI Belt for various uses.

CHUSI Large woven cloth (manta) used to carry products.

CHUSPA Woven bag used for carrying coca leaves.

GOLON Fringe along the borders of skirts.

HUGUNA Decorated bayeta blouse.

K'ALLU Half manta.

INTI The sun; a diamond-shaped motif representing the sun, commonly used in Bolivian weaving.

LLACOYA Rectangular handwoven cloth worn over a man's shoulders.

LLICLLA Square handwoven cloth worn over a woman's shoulders; carrying cloth. (Same as awayo.)

LLOQ'E Yarn spun to the left or with the left hand; Z-twisted yarn.

MANTA General term for any cloth.

MAQUITON Sleeves with borders and decorations worn only for major festivals.

MONTERA Circular hat—the various forms denote a particular community.

P'ALICHA O CULIS Small belt worn by children.

PAMPA The undecorated part of a cloth.

P'ANTA Woman's headcloth which hangs from the back of the head.

P'HULLO Small manta.

PICHI (See Topo.)

PONCHO Square or rectangular cloth with a central opening for the head.

PURILLA O POLLERA Wide skirt used by the women.

PUSHKA Drop spindle.

TOPO Silver, gold or copper pin used to fasten a woman's lliclla or awayo. (Same as Pichi.)

TULMA Man's or woman's hair-tie.

UNKHUÑA Small manta for coca leaves.

UNKU Tunic-like shirt; in some regions unku refers to a small cloth worn on the back or a pochito.

USUT'A Leather sandals.

VIRETE O CHULLO Hat with ear flaps and buttons.

WALTANA Belt used for swaddling babies. (Same as Empanadura.)

WATADO Warp ikat technique; derived from the Quechua word waytay, to tie or wrap.

WATANA Small woven ribbon with colourful fringes worn in the hair.

WAYAKA Small handwoven bag used to carry coca leaves and food stuffs.

WINCHA Woven headband adorned with glass beads, worn by the women of Charazani, Bolivia.

References

1. El Primer Nueva Coronica y Buen Gobierno
   (Siglo Veintiuno)
   Felipe Guaman Poma de Ayala (16th Century)
   Instituto de Estudios Peruanos

2. The Symbolism of the Figurative Belt in the Peruvian Sierra
   Gertrud B. de Solari
   Unpublished, June 1985

3. Genesis de la Cultura Andina
   Carlos Milla Villena
   Fondo Editorial C.A.P. Coleccion Bienal

4. Arte y Tesoros del Peru — Huari
   Jose Antonio de Lavalle
   Banco de Credito del Peru en la Cultura

5. Arte y Tesoros del Peru — Chavin
   Jose Antonio de Lavalle, Werner Lang
   Banco de Credito del Peru en la Cultura

6. Arte y Tesoros del Peru — Chancay
   Jose Antonio de Lavalle, Werner Lang
   Banco de Credito del Peru en la Cultura

7. Arte y Tesoros del Peru — Paracas
   Jose Antonio de Lavalle, Werner Lang
   Banco de Credito del Peru en la Cultura

8. Arte y Tesoros del Peru — Arte Precolombino
   Jose Antonio de Lavalle, Werner Lang
   Banco de Credito del Peru en la Cultura

9. Textiles of Ancient Peru and their Techniques
   Raoul D'Harcourt
   University of Washington Press
   *(Recommended for serious study of pre-Colombian techniques)

10. Tintes Naturales
    Hugo Zumbuhl
    Kamaq Maki Co-operative, Huancayo, Peru

11. Aymara Weavings
    (Ceremonial Textiles of Colonial and 19th Century Bolivia)
    L. Adelston & A. Tracht
    Smithsonian Institute

12. Disenos Precolombinos del Peru
    Yoshitaro Amano
    Museo Amano

13. Vestido Tradicional del Peru
    Luisa Castenada Leon
    Museo Nacional de le Cultura Peruana